Eighth International Joint Conference on Natural Language Processing (IJCNLP 2017)

Tutorial Abstracts

Taipei, Taiwan
1 December 2017

ISBN: 978-1-5108-5296-9

Printed from e-media with permission by:

Curran Associates, Inc.
57 Morehouse Lane
Red Hook, NY 12571

Some format issues inherent in the e-media version may also appear in this print version.

Printed by Curran Associates, Inc. (2017)

For permission requests, please contact the Association for Computational Linguistics at the address below.

Association for Computational Linguistics
209 N. Eighth Street
Stroudsburg, Pennsylvania 18360

Phone: 1-570-476-8006
Fax: 1-570-476-0860

acl@aclweb.org

Additional copies of this publication are available from:

Curran Associates, Inc.
57 Morehouse Lane
Red Hook, NY 12571 USA
Phone: 845-758-0400
Fax: 845-758-2633
Email: curran@proceedings.com
Web: www.proceedings.com

IJCNLP 2017

The Eighth International Joint Conference on Natural Language Processing

Proceedings of the IJCNLP 2017, Tutorial Abstracts

November 27 December 1, 2017
Taipei, Taiwan

Introduction

A total of 9 tutorial proposals were submitted to the IJCNLP 2017 Tutorials track from which six were finally accepted. We are grateful to the IJCNLP community for the diverse, and high-quality proposals we received. This guarantees a strong tutorials track at IJCNLP 2017, but at the same time made the selection process very difficult. All proposals were reviewed by the chairs with assistance by colleagues and experts from the NLP community where necessary. The final selection was approved by the IJCNLP 2017 General Chair.

The following criteria guided the selection: (1) Quality: content, scope and organization of the proposal, competence and experience of the presenters. (2) Diversity: We tried to include diverse topics ranging from linguistically motivated approaches to current developments in deep learning. We would like to emphasize that we also selected one tutorial on how to improve scientific presentatons. We believe that our whole community – presenters and audience alike – will benefit from this tutorial. (3) Novelty: Tutorials recently held at similar events were not selected.

We would like to thank all the presenters for putting a lot of effort in the tutorials. We are indebted to the Local Chairs, the Publication Chairs and the IJCNLP 2017 General Chair for making it happen.

Enjoy,

Sadao Kurohashi, Kyoto University
Michael Strube, Heidelberg Institute for Theoretical Studies gGmbH
IJCNLP 2017 Tutorial Chairs

Tutorial chairs:

Sadao Kurohashi, Kyoto University
Michael Strube, Heidelberg Institute for Theoretical Studies gGmbH

Table of Contents

Conference Program

Monday, November 27, 2017

Morning Session

9:00–12:30 *Deep Learning in Lexical Analysis and Parsing*
Wanxiang Che and Yue Zhang

9:00–12:30 *Multilingual Vector Representations of Words, Sentences, and Documents*
Gerard de Melo

9:00–12:30 *Open-Domain Neural Dialogue Systems*
Yun-Nung Chen and Jianfeng Gao

Afternoon Session

13:30–17:00 *Neural Machine Translation: Basics, Practical Aspects and Recent Trends*
Fabien Cromieres, Toshiaki Nakazawa and Raj Dabre

13:30–17:00 *The Ultimate Presentation Makeup Tutorial: How to Polish your Posters, Slides and Presentations Skills*
Gustavo Paetzold and Lucia Specia

13:30–17:00 *The Challenge of Composition in Distributional and Formal Semantics*
Ran Tian, Koji Mineshima and Pascual Martínez-Gómez

Deep Learning in Lexical Analysis and Parsing

Wanxiang Che
Harbin Institute of Technology
car@ir.hit.edu.cn

Yue Zhang
Singapore University of Technology and Design
yue_zhang@sutd.edu.sg

Abstract

Lexical analysis and parsing tasks, modeling deeper properties of the words and their relationships to each other, typically involve word segmentation, part-of-speech tagging and parsing. A typical characteristic of such tasks is that the outputs have structured. All of them can fall into three types of structured prediction problems: sequence segmentation, sequence labeling and parsing.

In this tutorial, we will introduce two state-of-the-art methods to solve these structured prediction problems: graph-based and transition-based methods. While, traditional graph-based and transition-based methods depend on "feature engineering" work, which costs lots of human labor and may misses many useful features. Deep learning just right can overcome the above "feature engineering" problem. We will further introduction those deep learning models which have been successfully used for both graph-based and transition-based structured prediction.

1 Tutorial Overview

Lexical analysis and parsing tasks, modeling deeper properties of the words and their relationships to each other, typically involve word segmentation, part-of-speech tagging and parsing. A typical characteristic of such tasks is that the outputs have structured. All of them can fall into three types of structured prediction problems: sequence segmentation, sequence labeling and parsing. Because of the pervasive problem of ambiguity, none of the above problems are trivial to predict.

Two different methods have been used to solve these structured prediction problems, including graph-based methods and transition-based methods. The former differentiates output structures based on their characteristics directly, while the latter transforms output construction processes into state transition processes, differentiating sequences of transition actions.

The conditional random fields (CRFs) are typical graph-based methods, which aim to maximize the probability of the correct output structure. The graph-based methods can also be applied to dependency parsing, where the aim change to maximize the score of the correct output structure.

At the beginning, the transition-based methods were applied into dependency parsing. Latter, it was found that sequence segmentation and labeling can also be modeled into a sequence of state transition.

Both graph-based and transition-based methods depend on "feature engineering" work, that is huge hand-crafted features and their combination should be designed according to different tasks. It usually cost lots of human labor. More seriously, many useful features may be missed by human beings. The features extracted from training data also lack in generalization.

Neural networks, also with a fancy name deep learning, just right can overcome the above "feature engineering" problem. In theory, they can use non-linear activation functions and multiple layers to automatically find useful features. The novel network structures, such as convolutional or recurrent, help to reduce the difficulty further.

These deep learning models have been successfully used for both graph-based and transition-based structured prediction. In this tutorial, we will give a review of each line of work, by contrasting them with traditional statistical methods, and organizing them in consistent orders.

Proceedings of the The 8th International Joint Conference on Natural Language Processing, pages 1–2,
Taipei, Taiwan, November 27 – December 1, 2017.

2 Outline

1. Typical Lexical Analysis and Parsing Tasks
    - Word segmentation
    - POS tagging
    - Parsing
    - Structured Prediction
        - Sequence Segmentation
        - Sequence Labeling
        - Parsing
2. Deep Learning Background
    - Multilayer Perceptron (MLP)
    - Back-propagation
    - Word Embedding
    - Recurrent Neural Networks (RNNs)
    - Recursive Neural Networks
    - Convolutional Neural Networks (CNNs)
3. State-of-the-art Methods
    - Graph-based Methods
        - Conditional Random Fields
        - Graph-based Dependency Parsing
    - Transition-based Methods
        - Greedy Shift-Reduce Dependency Parsing
        - Greedy Sequence Labeling
        - Beam-search Training and Decoding
4. Neural Graph-based Methods
    - Neural Conditional Random Fields
    - Neural Graph-based Dependency Parsing
5. Neural Transition-based Methods
    - Neural Greedy Shift-Reduce Dependency Parsing
    - Neural Greedy Sequence Labeling
    - Globally Optimized Models

3 Instructors

Wanxiang Che is currently an associate professor of school of computer science and technology at Harbin Institute of Technology (HIT) and visiting associate professor of Stanford University (at NLP group in 2012). His main research area lies in Natural Language Processing (NLP). He currently leads a national natural science foundation of China, a national 973 and a number of research projects. He has published more than 40 papers in high level journals and conferences, and published two textbooks. He and his team have achieved good results in a number of international technical evaluations, such as the first place of CoNLL 2009 and the fourth place of CoNLL 2017. He was an area co-chair of ACL 2016, publication co-chairs of ACL 2015 and EMNLP 2011. The Language Technology Platform (LTP), an open source Chinese NLP system he leads to develop, has been authorized to more than 600 institutes and individuals including Baidu, Tencent and so on. He achieved the outstanding paper award honorable mention of AAAI 2013, the first prize of technological progress award in Heilongjiang province in 2016, Google focused research award in 2015 and 2016, the first prize of Hanwang youth innovation award and first prize of the Qian Weichan Chinese information processing science and technology award in 2010.

Yue Zhang is currently an assistant professor at Singapore University of Technology and Design. Before joining SUTD in July 2012, he worked as a postdoctoral research associate in University of Cambridge, UK. Yue Zhang received his DPhil and MSc degrees from University of Oxford, UK, and his BEng degree from Tsinghua University, China. His research interests include natural language processing, machine learning and artificial Intelligence. He has been working on statistical parsing, parsing, text synthesis, machine translation, sentiment analysis and stock market analysis intensively. Yue Zhang serves as the reviewer for top journals such as Computational Linguistics, Transaction of Association of Computational Linguistics (standing review committee) and Journal of Artificial Intelligence Research. He is the associate editor for ACM Transactions on Asian and Low Resource Language Information Processing. He is also PC member for conferences such as ACL, COLING, EMNLP, NAACL, EACL, AAAI and IJCAI. He was the area chairs of COLING 2014, NAACL 2015, EMNLP 2015, ACL 2017 and EMNLP 2017. He is the TPC chair of IALP 2017.

Multilingual Vector Representations of Words, Sentences, and Documents

Gerard de Melo
Department of Computer Science
Rutgers University – New Brunswick
gdm@demelo.org

Abstract

Neural vector representations are now ubiquitous in all subfields of natural language processing and text mining. While methods such as word2vec and GloVe are well-known, *multilingual* and *cross-lingual* vector representations have also become important. In particular, such representations can not only describe words, but also of entire sentences and documents as well.

1 Introduction

Vector representations are ubiquitous in all subfields of natural language processing and text mining. Well-known neural methods such as word2vec and GloVe enable us to obtain distributed vector representations of words, overcoming some of the sparsity issues faced by traditional distributional semantics methods. Such representations are learnt from co-occurrence information drawn from large monolingual corpora.

Oftentimes, however, we are interested in representations that enable us to transition across language boundaries. Thus, it is useful to consider *multilingual* vector representations, covering multiple languages, and in particular *cross lingual* vector representations, which capture the semantics of different items in the same vector space, even when said items stem from different source languages.

This is useful for representations of individual words (Section 2), but also of entire sentences (Section 3) and documents (Section 4) as well.

2 Multilingual Word Vectors

One can distinguish several broad classes of algorithms for inducing cross-lingual word vectors.

Projection Approaches. The first strategy is to train multiple separate vector spaces using standard methods and then align them cross-lingually. The latter can be achieved using techniques such as linear projections (Mikolov et al., 2013), Canonical Correlation Analysis (Faruqui and Dyer, 2014), or the approach by Gouws et al. (2015).

Parallel Corpora Approaches. The second strategy is to rely on parallel corpora and directly optimize a cross-lingual objective that considers sentence translations. Examples include the methods proposed by Klementiev et al. (2012), Kočiský et al. (2014), and Gouws and Søgaard (2015). Some of these simply use aligned sentences, while others require word alignments. Vulić and Moens (2015a) showed that comparable documents may suffice to learn bilingual embeddings.

External Supervision. Alternatively, a third strategy is to draw on supplementary sources of supervision. For this, one can extract more explicit semantic information from text and then incorporate the mined knowledge into the objective function (Chen and de Melo, 2015; Chen et al., 2016). Loza Mencía et al. (2016) propose exploiting document labels as a surrogate form of supervision for higher-quality embeddings.

Finally, one can also draw on lexical knowledge graphs such as WordNet and its multilingual extensions (de Melo and Weikum, 2010), or on Wikipedia (de Melo and Weikum, 2014). These resources provide a rich source of information to induce massively multilingual word vectors covering hundreds of languages in the same space (de Melo, 2015; de Melo, 2017), with the additional advantage of also yielding sense- or concept-specific representations.

3 Multilingual Sentence Vectors

Next, we turn to vector representations of sentences.

Proceedings of the The 8th International Joint Conference on Natural Language Processing, pages 3–5,
Taipei, Taiwan, November 27 – December 1, 2017. ©2017 AFNLP

Word Vector-inspired Approaches. A widely used strategy is to simply average the word vectors of words in a given sentence. Despite its simplicity, this method often works surprisingly well (Wieting et al., 2015; Arora et al., 2017).

An early attempt to incorporate sentences more explicitly into the objective function was proposed with the Paragraph Vectors approach (Le and Mikolov, 2014). This method is also occasionally referred to as doc2vec, as it straightforwardly extends word2vec to additionally create representations of sentences or other longer units. Several authors have devised bilingual variants of the Paragraph Vector approach (Pham et al., 2015; Mogadala and Rettinger, 2016).

The Skip-Thought Vector approach (Kiros et al., 2015), while also inspired by the word2vec skip-gram method, instead draws on recurrent units to encode and decode sentence representations such that the resulting representations are optimized for predicting neighbouring sentences.

External Supervision. Wieting et al. (2015) explored using supervision from paraphrase information to obtain custom-tailored word vectors that give rise to high-quality sentence embeddings. The InferSent approach (Conneau et al., 2017) relies on supervision from the Stanford Natural Language Inference data as an auxiliary task to obtain sentence representations. In terms of cross-lingual methods, neural machine translation based on sequence-to-sequence learning can give rise to vector encodings of multilingual input sentences (Luong et al., 2015). These have been shown to be semantically meaningful (Schwenk and Douze, 2017).

4 Multilingual Document Vectors

Finally, we consider representations of entire text documents.

Word Vector-inspired Approaches. To obtain document representations, a common choice is again to simply take the average of word vectors, or a suitably weighted sum. In doing so, one can directly rely on multilingual word vectors to generate cross-lingual documents representations (Klementiev et al., 2012) that can be used for tasks such as cross-lingual text classification (de Melo and Siersdorfer, 2007).

A fallback strategy is to translate all documents to a single language and then consider monolingual document similarity metrics. This approach may be more costly in terms of the resources used, and may neglect language-specific subtleties. Still, in practice, it does appear to be a strong baseline (de Melo and Siersdorfer, 2007).

Modeling Document Semantics. While many methods treat sentences and documents as interchangeable, there are significant differences between the two. Methods that focus specifically on properties of documents have the potential to yield higher-quality document-level embeddings. Bag-of-words vectors can be rendered cross-lingual by translating individual words (Song et al., 2016), or by moving from original words to bag-of-concept representations (de Melo and Siersdorfer, 2007), optionally drawing on distributed vectors for concepts (de Melo, 2017). Representations may also account for the salience of different parts of the text (Yang et al., 2016, 2017). Hermann and Blunsom (2014) train a siamese-style network architecture on a parallel corpus such that it learns to compose sentence representations into document representations. Finally, when documents are to be compared against short queries, it is important to consider the peculiarities of relevance modeling (Vulić and Moens, 2015b; Hui et al., 2017), which differs from semantic similarity modeling.

5 Conclusion

In summary, vector representations have made it easier to target multilingual and cross-lingual semantics. This is possible both at the level of individual words as well as at the level of sentences or even entire documents.

Biography

Gerard de Melo is an Assistant Professor of Computer Science at Rutgers University, heading a team of researchers working on NLP, Big Data analytics, and web mining. He has published over 80 papers on these topics, with Best Paper/Demo awards at WWW 2011, CIKM 2010, ICGL 2008, the NAACL 2015 Workshop on Vector Space Modeling, as well as an ACL 2014 Best Paper Honorable Mention, a Best Student Paper Award nomination at ESWC 2015, and a thesis award for his work on graph algorithms for knowledge modeling. Notable research projects include UWN/MENTA, the first massively multilingual version of WordNet, and Lexvo.org, an important hub in the Web of Data. For further information, please refer to `http://gerard.demelo.org`.

References

Sanjeev Arora, Yingyu Liang, and Tengyu Ma. 2017. A simple but tough-to-beat baseline for sentence embeddings. In *Proceedings of ICLR 2017*.

Jiaqiang Chen and Gerard de Melo. 2015. Semantic information extraction for improved word embeddings. In *Proceedings of the NAACL Workshop on Vector Space Modeling for NLP*.

Jiaqiang Chen, Niket Tandon, Charles Darwis Hariman, and Gerard de Melo. 2016. WebBrain: Joint neural learning of large-scale commonsense knowledge. In *Proceedings of ISWC 2016*.

Alexis Conneau, Douwe Kiela, Holger Schwenk, Loïc Barrault, and Antoine Bordes. 2017. Supervised learning of universal sentence representations from natural language inference data. *CoRR*, abs/1705.02364.

Gerard de Melo. 2015. Wiktionary-based word embeddings. In *Proceedings of MT Summit XV*. AMTA.

Manaal Faruqui and Chris Dyer. 2014. Improving vector space word representations using multilingual correlation. In *Proceedings of EACL 2014*.

Stephan Gouws, Yoshua Bengio, and Greg Corrado. 2015. BilBOWA: Fast bilingual distributed representations without word alignments. In *Proceedings of ICML 2015*.

Stephan Gouws and Anders Søgaard. 2015. Simple task-specific bilingual word embeddings. In *Proceedings of NAACL-HLT*.

Karl Moritz Hermann and Phil Blunsom. 2014. Multilingual models for compositional distributed semantics. In *Proceedings of ACL 2014*.

Kai Hui, Andrew Yates, Klaus Berberich, and Gerard de Melo. 2017. A position-aware deep model for relevance matching in information retrieval. In *Proceedings of EMNLP 2017*.

Ryan Kiros, Yukun Zhu, Ruslan Salakhutdinov, Richard S. Zemel, Antonio Torralba, Raquel Urtasun, and Sanja Fidler. 2015. Skip-thought vectors. In *Proceedings of NIPS 2015*. MIT Press.

Alexandre Klementiev, Ivan Titov, and Binod Bhattarai. 2012. Inducing crosslingual distributed representations of words. In *Proceedings of COLING*.

Tomáš Kočiský, Karl Moritz Hermann, and Phil Blunsom. 2014. Learning bilingual word representations by marginalizing alignments. In *Proceedings of ACL 2014*.

Quoc Le and Tomas Mikolov. 2014. Distributed representations of sentences and documents. In *Proceedings of ICML 2014*. PMLR.

Eneldo Loza Mencía, Gerard de Melo, and Jinseok Nam. 2016. Medical concept embeddings via labeled background corpora. In *Proceedings of LREC*.

Minh-Thang Luong, Quoc V. Le, Ilya Sutskever, Oriol Vinyals, and Lukasz Kaiser. 2015. Multi-task sequence to sequence learning. *CoRR*, abs/1511.06114.

Gerard de Melo. 2017. Inducing conceptual embedding spaces from Wikipedia. In *Proceedings of WWW 2017*. ACM.

Gerard de Melo and Stefan Siersdorfer. 2007. Multilingual text classification using ontologies. In *Proceedings of ECIR 2007*, volume 4425 of *LNCS*. Springer.

Gerard de Melo and Gerhard Weikum. 2010. Towards universal multilingual knowledge bases. In *Proceedings of the 5th Global WordNet Conference*.

Gerard de Melo and Gerhard Weikum. 2014. Taxonomic data integration from multilingual Wikipedia editions. *Knowledge and Information Systems*, 39(1):1–39.

Tomas Mikolov, Ilya Sutskever, Kai Chen, Greg Corrado, and Jeffrey Dean. 2013. Distributed representations of words and phrases and their compositionality. In *Proceedings of NIPS 2013*.

Aditya Mogadala and Achim Rettinger. 2016. Bilingual word embeddings from parallel and non-parallel corpora for cross-language text classification. In *Proceedings of NAACL 2016*.

Hieu Pham, Minh-Thang Luong, and Christopher D Manning. 2015. Learning distributed representations for multilingual text sequences. In *Proceedings of NAACL-HLT 2015*.

Holger Schwenk and Matthijs Douze. 2017. Learning joint multilingual sentence representations with neural machine translation. In *Proceedings of the 2nd Workshop on Representation Learning for NLP*.

Yangqiu Song, Shyam Upadhyay, Haoruo Peng, and Dan Roth. 2016. Cross-lingual dataless classification for many languages. In *Proceedings of IJCAI*.

Ivan Vulić and Marie-Francine Moens. 2015a. Bilingual word embeddings from non-parallel document-aligned data applied to bilingual lexicon induction. In *Proceedings of ACL-IJCNLP 2015*.

Ivan Vulić and Marie-Francine Moens. 2015b. Monolingual and cross-lingual information retrieval models based on (bilingual) word embeddings. In *Proceedings of SIGIR 2015*. ACM.

John Wieting, Mohit Bansal, Kevin Gimpel, and Karen Livescu. 2015. Towards universal paraphrastic sentence embeddings. *CoRR*, abs/1511.08198.

Qian Yang, Yong Cheng, Sen Wang, and Gerard de Melo. 2017. HiText: Text reading with dynamic salience marking. In *Proceedings of WWW 2017*.

Qian Yang, Rebecca J. Passonneau, and Gerard de Melo. 2016. PEAK: Pyramid evaluation via automated knowledge extraction. In *Proceedings of AAAI*.

Open-Domain Neural Dialogue Systems

Yun-Nung Chen
National Taiwan University
Taipei, Taiwan
y.v.chen@ieee.org

Jianfeng Gao
Microsoft AI & Research
Redmond, WA
jfgao@microsoft.com

1 Tutorial Overview

Until recently, the goal of developing open-domain dialogue systems that not only emulate human conversation but fulfill complex tasks, such as travel planning, seemed elusive. However, we start to observe promising results in the last few years as the large amount of conversation data is available for training and the breakthroughs in deep learning and reinforcement learning are applied to dialogue. In this tutorial, we start with a brief introduction to the history of dialogue research. Then, we describe in detail the deep learning and reinforcement learning technologies that have been developed for two types of dialogue systems. First is a task-oriented dialogue system that can help users accomplish tasks, ranging from meeting scheduling to vacation planning. Second is a social bot that can converse seamlessly and appropriately with humans. In the final part of the tutorial, we review attempts to developing open-domain neural dialogue systems by combining the strengths of task-oriented dialogue systems and social bots. The tutorial material is available at http://opendialogue.miulab.tw.

2 Outline

1. Introduction & Background [15 min.]
   - Brief history of dialogue research
   - Challenges of developing dialogue agents
   - Task-oriented dialogue systems
   - Social chat bots
   - How to evaluate dialogue systems
   - Neural network basics
   - Reinforcement learning (RL) basics
2. Task-Oriented Dialogue System [75 min.]
   - Natural language understanding (NLU)
     - Domain and intent classification
     - Slot tagging
     - Joint semantic frame parsing
     - Contextual language understanding
     - Structural language understanding
   - Dialogue management (DM) – Dialogue state tracking (DST)
     - Neural belief tracker
     - Multichannel tracker
   - Dialogue management (DM) – Dialogue policy optimization
     - Dialogue RL signal
     - Deep Q-network for learning policy
     - Hierarchical RL for learning policy
   - Natural language generation (NLG)
     - Rule-based NLG
     - Learning-based NLG
     - Structural NLG
     - Contextual NLG
   - End-to-end task-oriented dialogue systems
     - Joint learning of NLU and DM
     - Supervised learning for dialogues
     - Memory networks for dialogues
     - RL-based *InfoBot*
     - LSTM-based dialogue control
     - RL-based task-completion bots
3. Social Chat Bots [75 min.]
   - Neural response generation models
   - Making the response diverse
   - Making the response consistent
   - Deep reinforcement learning for response generation
   - Image-grounded response generation
   - Knowledge-grounded response generation
   - Generative seq2seq for task-oriented dialogues
   - Combining task-oriented bots and social bots
4. Challenges & Conclusions [15 mins]

Proceedings of the The 8th International Joint Conference on Natural Language Processing, pages 6–10,
Taipei, Taiwan, November 27 – December 1, 2017. ©2017 AFNLP

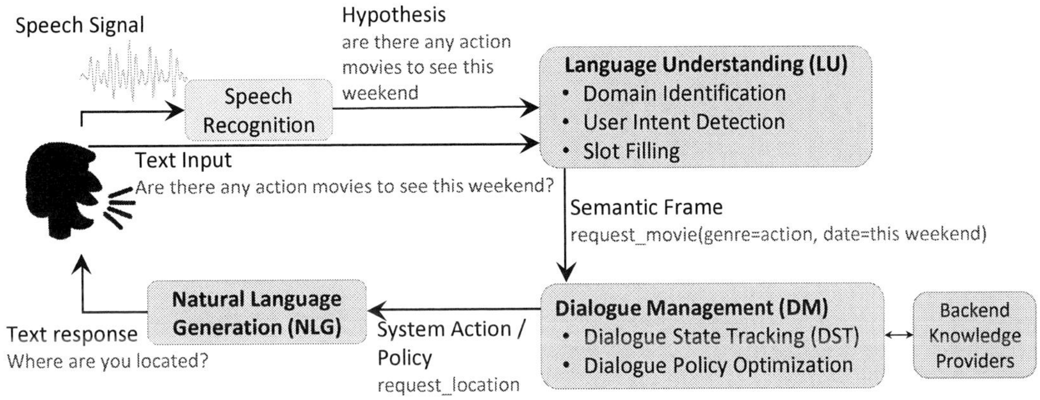

Figure 1: Pipeline framework of task-oriented dialog system.

3 Task-Oriented Dialogue Systems

The architecture of a task-oriented dialogue system is illustrated in Figure 1 (Tur and De Mori, 2011). It consists of three components, natural language understanding (NLU), dialogue management (DM), and natural language generation (NLG) (Rudnicky et al., 1999; Zue et al., 2000; Zue and Glass, 2000).

Natural Language Understanding NLU traditionally consists of domain identification and intent prediction, which are framed as utterance classification problems, and slot filling, framed as a sequence tagging task.

With the advances on deep learning, recent development has been focused on neural approaches. Ravuri and Stolcke (2015) proposed an RNN architecture for intent determination. Xu and Sarikaya (2013) incoporated features generated using neural approaches into the CRF framework for slot filling. Yao et al. (2013) and Mesnil et al. (2015) later employed soly the RNN-based sequence labeling model for slot filling. Such an architecture has been further extended to jointly model intent detection and slot filling in multiple domains (Hakkani-Tür et al., 2016; Jaech et al., 2016). End-to-end memory networks have shown to provide a good mechanism for integrating global knowledge context and local dialogue context into these models (Chen et al., 2016a,b). In addition, the importance of the NLU module is investigated in Li et al. (2017a), showing that different types of errors from NLU can degrade the whole system's performance in a reinforcement learning setting.

Dialogue Management DM plays two roles, tracking the dialogue state and performing the dialogue policy (i.e., telling the agent how to act given the dialogue state.)

The state-of-the-art dialogue managers monitor the dialogue progress (state) using neural dialogue state tracking models (Henderson et al., 2013). Recent work shows that that Neural Dialog Managers provide conjoint representations between the utterances, slot-value pairs as well as knowledge graph representations (Wen et al., 2016; Mrkšić et al., 2016; Liu and Lane, 2017), and thus make the deployment of large-scale dialogue systems for complex domain much easier.

A partially observable Markov decision process (POMDP) has been shown to be an effective mathematical framework for dialogue policy learning since it can model the uncertainty such as those caused by speech recognition errors and semantic decoding errors (Williams and Young, 2007; Young et al., 2013). Under POMDP, dialogue policy is trained using reinforcement learning (RL) where the agent learns how to act based on the reward signals recieved from the environment (Sutton and Barto, 1998).

Natural Language Generation NLG approaches can be grouped into two categories, one focuses on generating text using templates or rules (linguistic) methods, the other uses corpus-based statistical methods (Oh and Rudnicky, 2002).

The RNN-based models have been applied to language generation for both social bots and task-orientated dialogue systems (Sordoni et al., 2015; Vinyals and Le, 2015; Wen et al., 2015b). The RNN-based NLG can learn from unaligned

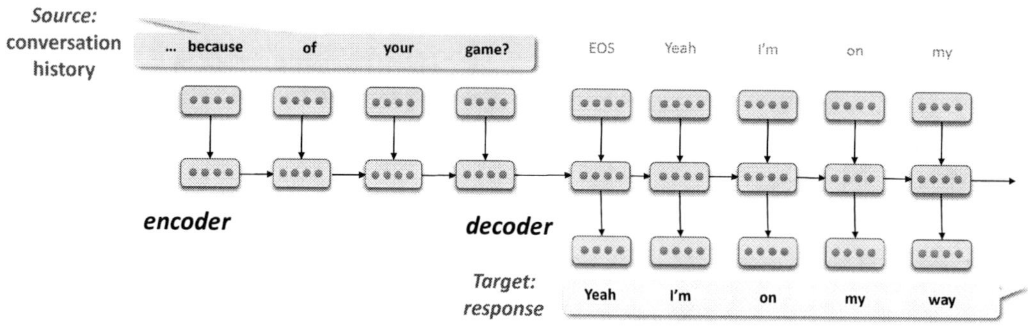

Figure 2: Illustration of a sequence-to-sequence model for chit-chat dialogues.

data by jointly optimizing sentence planning and surface realization, and language variation can be achieved by sampling from output candidates (Wen et al., 2015a). Moreover, Wen et al. (2015b) improved the prior work by adding a gating mechanism to control the dialogue act during generation in order to avoid repetition.

End-to-End Task-Oriented Dialogue System Awaring the representation power of deep neural networks, there are more and more attempts to learning dialogue systems in an end-to-end fashion using different learning frameworks, including supervised learning and reinforcement learning (Yang et al., 2017).

Wen et al. (2016) and Bordes and Weston (2016) introduced a network-based end-to-end trainable task-oriented dialogue system. The authors treated training a dialogue system as learning a mapping from dialogue histories to system responses, and applied an encoder-decoder model.However, the system is trained in a supervised fashion that requires a lot of training data. Thus, the agent cannot learn a robust dialogue policy since it never explore the unknown space that is not covered by the limited training data.

Zhao and Eskenazi (2016) presented an end-to-end reinforcement learning (RL) approach to dialogue state tracking and policy learning. They show some promising results when applying the agent to the task of guessing the famous person a user is thinking of. Dhingra et al. (2017) proposed an end-to-end differentiable KB-Infobot for efficient information access. Li et al. (2017b) presented an end-to-end neural dialogue system for task completion. The agent can handle a wide varity of question types, including user-initated request.

4 Social Chat Bots

Social bots are of growing importance in facilitating smooth interaction between humans and their electronic devices. Recently, researcher have begun to explore data-driven generation of conversational responses within the framework of nerual machine translation (NMT) in the form of encoder-decoder or seq2seq models (Sordoni et al., 2015; Vinyals and Le, 2015; Li et al., 2016a), as illustrated in Figure 2.

However, the generated responses are often too general to carry meaningful information, such as "I don't know.", which can serve as a response to any user questions. A mutual information based model was proposed to address the issue, a mutual information model is proposed by Li et al. (2016a), and is later improved by using deep reinforcement learning (Li et al., 2016c). Furthermore, Li et al. (2016b) presented a persona-based model to address the issue of speaker consistency in neural response generation.

Although task-oriented dialogue systems and social bots are originally developed for different purposes, there is a trend of combining both as a step towards building an open-domain dialogue agent.

For example, on the one hand, Ghazvininejad et al. (2017) presented a fully data-driven and knowledge-grounded neural conversation model aimed at producing more contentful responses without slot filling. On the other hand, Zhao et al. (2017) proposed a task-oriented dialogue agented based on the encoder-decoder model with chatting capability.

5 Instructors

Yun-Nung (Vivian) Chen is currently an assistant professor at the Department of Computer Science, National Taiwan University. She earned her Ph.D. degree from Carnegie Mellon University, where her research interests focus on spoken dialogue system, language understanding, natural language processing, and multi-modal speech applications. She received the Google Faculty Research Awards 2016, two Student Best Paper Awards from IEEE SLT 2010 and IEEE ASRU 2013, a Student Best Paper Nominee from Interspeech 2012, and the Distinguished Master Thesis Award from ACLCLP. Before joining National Taiwan University, she worked in the Deep Learning Technology Center at Microsoft Research Redmond. More information about her can be found at `http://vivianchen.idv.tw`.

Jianfeng Gao is Partner Research Manager in Business AI at Microsoft AI and Research. From 2014 to 2017, he was Partner Research Manager and Principal Researcher at Deep Learning Technology Center at MSR Redmond. He leads the development of AI solutions to Predictive Sales and Marketing. Gao also works on deep learning for text and image processing and leads the development of AI systems for dialogue, machine reading comprehension, and question answering. From 2006 to 2014, he was a principal researcher at NLP Group at MSR Redmond, working on Web search, query understanding and reformulation, ads prediction, and statistical machine translation. From 2005 to 2006, Gao was a research lead in Natural Interactive Services Division at Microsoft, working on Project X, an effort of developing natural user interface for Windows. From 1999 to 2005, Gao was a research lead in Natural Language Computing Group at MSR Asia, developing the first Chinese speech recognition system released with Microsoft Office, the Chinese/Japanese Input Method Editors which were the leading products in the market, and the natural language platform for Windows Vista. More information can be found at `https://www.microsoft.com/en-us/research/people/jfgao/`.

References

Antoine Bordes and Jason Weston. 2016. Learning end-to-end goal-oriented dialog. *arXiv preprint arXiv:1605.07683*.

Yun-Nung Chen, Dilek Hakkani-Tur, Gokhan Tur, Asli Celikyilmaz, Jianfeng Gao, and Li Deng. 2016a. Knowledge as a teacher: Knowledge-guided structural attention networks. *arXiv preprint arXiv:1609.03286*.

Yun-Nung Chen, Dilek Hakkani-Tür, Gokhan Tur, Jianfeng Gao, and Li Deng. 2016b. End-to-end memory networks with knowledge carryover for multi-turn spoken language understanding. In *Proceedings of the Interspeech*.

Bhuwan Dhingra, Lihong Li, Xiujun Li, Jianfeng Gao, Yun-Nung Chen, Faisal Ahmed, and Li Deng. 2017. Towards end-to-end reinforcement learning of dialogue agents for information access. pages 484–495.

Marjan Ghazvininejad, Chris Brockett, Ming-Wei Chang, Bill Dolan, Jianfeng Gao, Wen-tau Yih, and Michel Galley. 2017. A knowledge-grounded neural conversation model. *arXiv preprint arXiv:1702.01932*.

Dilek Hakkani-Tür, Gokhan Tur, Asli Celikyilmaz, Yun-Nung Chen, Jianfeng Gao, Li Deng, and Ye-Yi Wang. 2016. Multi-domain joint semantic frame parsing using bi-directional RNN-LSTM. In *Proceedings of the Interspeech*, San Francisco, CA.

Matthew Henderson, Blaise Thomson, and Steve Young. 2013. Deep neural network approach for the dialog state tracking challenge. In *Proceedings of the SIGDIAL 2013 Conference*, pages 467–471.

A. Jaech, L. Heck, and M. Ostendorf. 2016. Domain adaptation of recurrent neural networks for natural language understanding. In *Proceedings of the Interspeech*, San Francisco, CA.

Jiwei Li, Michel Galley, Chris Brockett, Jianfeng Gao, and Bill Dolan. 2016a. A diversity-promoting objective function for neural conversation models. In *Proceedings of NAACL-HLT*, pages 110–119.

Jiwei Li, Michel Galley, Chris Brockett, Georgios P Spithourakis, Jianfeng Gao, and Bill Dolan. 2016b. A persona-based neural conversation model. In *Proceedings of ACL*.

Jiwei Li, Will Monroe, Alan Ritter, Michel Galley, Jianfeng Gao, and Dan Jurafsky. 2016c. Deep reinforcement learning for dialogue generation. In *Proceedings of EMNLP*.

Xiujun Li, Yun-Nung Chen, Lihong Li, Jianfeng Gao, and Asli Celikyilmaz. 2017a. Investigation of language understanding impact for reinforcement learning based dialogue systems. *arXiv preprint arXiv:1703.07055*.

Xuijun Li, Yun-Nung Chen, Lihong Li, Jianfeng Gao, and Asli Celikyilmaz. 2017b. End-to-end task-completion neural dialogue systems. In *Proceedings of IJCNLP*.

Bing Liu and Ian Lane. 2017. An end-to-end trainable neural network model with belief tracking for task-oriented dialog. In *Proceedings of Interspeech*.

Grégoire Mesnil, Yann Dauphin, Kaisheng Yao, Yoshua Bengio, Li Deng, Dilek Hakkani-Tur, Xiaodong He, Larry Heck, Gokhan Tur, Dong Yu, et al. 2015. Using recurrent neural networks for slot filling in spoken language understanding. *IEEE/ACM Transactions on Audio, Speech, and Language Processing*, 23(3):530–539.

Nikola Mrkšić, Diarmuid Ó Séaghdha, Tsung-Hsien Wen, Blaise Thomson, and Steve Young. 2016. Neural belief tracker: Data-driven dialogue state tracking. *arXiv preprint arXiv:1606.03777*.

Alice H Oh and Alexander I Rudnicky. 2002. Stochastic natural language generation for spoken dialog systems. *Computer Speech & Language*, 16(3):387–407.

Suman Ravuri and Andreas Stolcke. 2015. Recurrent neural network and lstm models for lexical utterance classification. In *Sixteenth Annual Conference of the International Speech Communication Association*.

Alexander I Rudnicky, Eric H Thayer, Paul C Constantinides, Chris Tchou, R Shern, Kevin A Lenzo, Wei Xu, and Alice Oh. 1999. Creating natural dialogs in the carnegie mellon communicator system. In *Eurospeech*.

Alessandro Sordoni, Michel Galley, Michael Auli, Chris Brockett, Yangfeng Ji, Margaret Mitchell, Jian-Yun Nie, Jianfeng Gao, and Bill Dolan. 2015. A neural network approach to context-sensitive generation of conversational responses. In *Proceedings of NAACL-HLT*.

Richard S Sutton and Andrew G Barto. 1998. *Reinforcement learning: An introduction*, volume 1. MIT press Cambridge.

Gokhan Tur and Renato De Mori. 2011. *Spoken language understanding: Systems for extracting semantic information from speech*. John Wiley & Sons.

Oriol Vinyals and Quoc Le. 2015. A neural conversational model. *arXiv preprint arXiv:1506.05869*.

Tsung-Hsien Wen, Milica Gašic, Dongho Kim, Nikola Mrkšic, Pei-Hao Su, David Vandyke, and Steve Young. 2015a. Stochastic language generation in dialogue using recurrent neural networks with convolutional sentence reranking. In *16th Annual Meeting of the Special Interest Group on Discourse and Dialogue*, page 275.

Tsung-Hsien Wen, Milica Gasic, Nikola Mrksic, Lina M Rojas-Barahona, Pei-Hao Su, Stefan Ultes, David Vandyke, and Steve Young. 2016. A network-based end-to-end trainable task-oriented dialogue system. *arXiv preprint arXiv:1604.04562*.

Tsung-Hsien Wen, Milica Gasic, Nikola Mrksic, Pei-Hao Su, David Vandyke, and Steve Young. 2015b. Semantically conditioned lstm-based natural language generation for spoken dialogue systems. *arXiv preprint arXiv:1508.01745*.

Jason D Williams and Steve Young. 2007. Partially observable markov decision processes for spoken dialog systems. *Computer Speech & Language*, 21(2):393–422.

Puyang Xu and Ruhi Sarikaya. 2013. Convolutional neural network based triangular CRF for joint intent detection and slot filling. In *2013 IEEE Workshop on Automatic Speech Recognition and Understanding (ASRU)*, pages 78–83. IEEE.

Xuesong Yang, Yun-Nung Chen, Dilek Hakkani-Tür, Paul Crook, Xiujun Li, Jianfeng Gao, , and Li Deng. 2017. End-to-end joint learning of natural language understanding and dialogue manager. In *Proceedings of ICASSP*.

Kaisheng Yao, Geoffrey Zweig, Mei-Yuh Hwang, Yangyang Shi, and Dong Yu. 2013. Recurrent neural networks for language understanding. In *INTERSPEECH*, pages 2524–2528.

Steve Young, Milica Gašić, Blaise Thomson, and Jason D Williams. 2013. POMDP-based statistical spoken dialog systems: A review. *Proceedings of the IEEE*, 101(5):1160–1179.

Tiancheng Zhao and Maxine Eskenazi. 2016. Towards end-to-end learning for dialog state tracking and management using deep reinforcement learning. In *Proceedings of SIGDIAL*.

Tiancheng Zhao, Allen Lu, Kyusong Lee, and Maxine Eskenazi. 2017. Generative encoder-decoder models for task-oriented spoken dialog systems with chatting capability. In *Proceedings of SigDial*.

Victor Zue, Stephanie Seneff, James R Glass, Joseph Polifroni, Christine Pao, Timothy J Hazen, and Lee Hetherington. 2000. JUPITER: a telephone-based conversational interface for weather information. *IEEE Transactions on speech and audio processing*, 8(1):85–96.

Victor W Zue and James R Glass. 2000. Conversational interfaces: Advances and challenges. *Proceedings of the IEEE*, 88(8):1166–1180.

Neural Machine Translation: Basics, Practical Aspects and Recent Trends

Raj Dabre[1] **, Fabien Cromieres**[2], and **Toshiaki Nakazawa**[2]
[1]Graduate School of Informatics, Kyoto University
[2]Japan Science and Technology Agency
raj@nlp.ist.i.kyoto-u.ac.jp, fabien@nlp.ist.i.kyoto-u.ac.jp,
nakazawa@nlp.ist.i.kyoto-u.ac.jp

Abstract

In just a few years, Neural Machine Translation (NMT)(Bahdanau et al., 2015; Cho et al., 2014) has become the main approach to Machine Translation as well as one of the most successful application of Deep Learning to NLP. It leverages powerful machine learning techniques to train complex translation models in an end-to-end manner. Although this area of research is pretty new, the many recent developments combined with the practical difficulties of deep learning can make it difficult for a researcher lacking the background and practical experience to develop state-of-the-art models. This tutorial is aimed at people who want to conduct NMT research but have little prior experience in this field. We hope that by the end of the tutorial the audience will have a working understanding of the basics, practical aspects and the recent advancements in NMT.

1 Tutorial Overview

This tutorial is primarily aimed at researchers who are fairly new to the world of NMT and want to obtain a deep understanding of NMT fundamentals. Because it will also cover the latest developments in NMT, it should also be useful to attendees with more experience in NMT. Roughly half of the tutorial will be spent on understanding the working of the sequence-to-sequence encoder-decoder with attention mechanism. This model introduced in (Bahdanau et al., 2015) has become the de facto baseline model in MT research.

The latter half of this tutorial will cover some practical aspects of applying NMT models such as preprocessing (especially in the case of Asian languages), model training and translation search (decoding). Some of these practical aspects are rarely explicitely described, but are important when one wants to obtain state-of-the-art results. This will be followed by a fairly comprehensive review of the recent advancements and trends in NMT that constitute the state of the art, in particular the recent trend trying to replace the recurrent components with more computation-efficient feed-forward components (as in (Vaswani et al., 2017)). This half of the tutorial will be useful to both NMT beginners as well as those with a fair amount of experience.

2 Structure

1. **Introduction: The appearance of NMT in the Machine Translation world** (15 min)
   - A quick review of the evolution of the approaches to Machine Translation
   - Applications of NMT beyond translation (POS Tagging, Parsing, etc) (Vinyals et al., 2015) and related topics (Image Captioning).
2. **The Encoder-Decoder Model** (45 min)

   The objective of this part of the tutorial is to give an indepth explanation of the recurrent NMT model that uses attention. We will give enough details to make sure that the audience has a good working idea of the NMT model and be in a position to try and implement it by themselves.

   - The general architecture of the recurrent sequence-to-sequence model.
   - Background information and notations (including linear algebra needed to understand).
   - Quick overview of recurrent neural network basics (LSTMs, GRUs, etc).
   - Generic sequence to sequence model.

Proceedings of the The 8th International Joint Conference on Natural Language Processing, pages 11–13,
Taipei, Taiwan, November 27 – December 1, 2017.

- Encoder-Decoder model without attention and the results.
- Attention mechanism and its results and implications.
- Variations of attention mechanisms like local attention and various attention strategies (dot product, linear combination, etc) (Luong et al., 2015).
- Visualizations of attention mechanisms.
- Model training in an end to end fashion.
- Limitations of the current model (Unknown words, gradient propagation issues in stacked RNNs etc).

(EXTRA) Overview of implementations of the NMT models and the frameworks: KNMT[1], Lamtram[2], Open NMT[3], Nematus[4], Tensor2Tensor[5].

Coffee Break (30 min)

3. **Practical NMT** (45 min)

   The objective of this part of the tutorial is to augment the audience's understanding of NMT with various practical ideas that can help improve the quality and speed of NMT as well as showcase the many black box applications of NMT.

   - Preprocessing and management of rare words.
   - Subword units to enable infinite vocabulary.
   - BPE (Byte Pair Encoding) and its impact on translation quality (Sennrich et al., 2016b).
   - Using monolingual corpora to improve NMT (Gülçehre et al., 2015; Sennrich et al., 2016a).
   - Training and Translation search.
   - Optimization algorithms (ADAM etc).
   - Residual connections.
   - Training schedules for optimal results (ADAM –> SGD –> annealing –> early stopping).
   - Regularization, dropout and hyperparameter tuning to improve results.
   - Beam search, model averaging and ensembling.

4. **Recent Developments** (45 min)

   The objective of this part of the tutorial is to bring the audience up to speed with the current SOTA (state-of-the-art) NMT models and advancements. We plan to enumerate the most important ones and thereby provide the audience members a roadmap to understanding the big picture.

   - Facebook's CNN (Convolutional Neural Network) based NMT model (Gehring et al., 2017).
   - Google's Transformer (Vaswani et al., 2017) that replies purely on attention and feedforward networks (SOTA for WMT tasks).
   - Results and speedup in training achieved by these architectures.
   - Multilingual Multiway NMT (ML-NMT) (Firat et al., 2016) and Zero Shot NMT (Johnson et al., 2016).
   - Other advances (search-guided, latent graph, pointer networks)

5. **Summary and Conclusion**

3 About the Speakers

- **Raj Dabre**: Graduate School of Informatics, Kyoto University, Japan (raj@nlp.ist.i.kyoto-u.ac.jp)

  Raj Dabre is a 3rd year PhD student at Kyoto University. His research interests center on natural language processing, particularly neural machine translation for low resource languages and domain adaptation. He has MT-related publications in ACL, NAACL, COLING and WMT. He was a part of the organizing committee of COLING 2012 and has coordinated joint research between Kyoto University (Japan) and IIT Bombay (India).

- **Dr. Fabien Cromieres**: Japan Science and Technology Agency (JST), Japan (fabien@nlp.ist.i.kyoto-u.ac.jp)

  Fabien Cromieres is currently working with the Japan Science and Technology Agency in a project aiming at improve the translation of

[1] https://github.com/fabiencro/knmt
[2] https://github.com/neubig/lamtram
[3] http://opennmt.net
[4] https://github.com/EdinburghNLP/nematus
[5] https://github.com/tensorflow/tensor2tensor

technical documents between Japanese and Chinese. Initially focused on Example-Based Machine Translation, he has been working on Neural Machine Translation since the end of 2015. He is one of the authors of KyotoEBMT and KyotoNMT MT systems and has MT-related publications in EACL, NAACL, EMNLP and WAT.

- **Dr. Toshiaki Nakazawa**: Japan Science and Technology Agency (JST), Japan (nakazawa@nlp.ist.i.kyoto-u.ac.jp)

  Toshiaki Nakazawa is currently working for the Japan Science and Technology Agency (JST) as a researcher of Project on Practical Implementation of Japanese to Chinese and Chinese to Japanese Machine Translation. His research interests center on natural language processing, particularly language resource construction, linguistically motivated machine translation and NLP tools in human activities. He is one of the authors of KyotoEBMT and has MT-related publications in NAACL, EMNLP, COLING and WAT. He is also one of the organizers of the WAT workshops.

References

Dzmitry Bahdanau, Kyunghyun Cho, and Yoshua Bengio. 2015. Neural machine translation by jointly learning to align and translate. In *In Proceedings of the 3rd International Conference on Learning Representations (ICLR 2015)*, San Diego, USA. International Conference on Learning Representations.

Kyunghyun Cho, Bart van Merriënboer, ÇaÄ§lar Gülçehre, Dzmitry Bahdanau, Fethi Bougares, Holger Schwenk, and Yoshua Bengio. 2014. Learning phrase representations using rnn encoder–decoder for statistical machine translation. In *Proceedings of the 2014 Conference on Empirical Methods in Natural Language Processing (EMNLP)*, pages 1724–1734, Doha, Qatar. Association for Computational Linguistics.

Orhan Firat, Kyunghyun Cho, and Yoshua Bengio. 2016. Multi-way, multilingual neural machine translation with a shared attention mechanism. In *NAACL HLT 2016, The 2016 Conference of the North American Chapter of the Association for Computational Linguistics: Human Language Technologies, San Diego California, USA, June 12-17, 2016*, pages 866–875.

Jonas Gehring, Michael Auli, David Grangier, Denis Yarats, and Yann N Dauphin. 2017. Convolutional Sequence to Sequence Learning. *ArXiv e-prints*.

Çaglar Gülçehre, Orhan Firat, Kelvin Xu, Kyunghyun Cho, Loïc Barrault, Huei-Chi Lin, Fethi Bougares, Holger Schwenk, and Yoshua Bengio. 2015. On using monolingual corpora in neural machine translation. *CoRR*, abs/1503.03535.

Melvin Johnson, Mike Schuster, Quoc V. Le, Maxim Krikun, Yonghui Wu, Zhifeng Chen, Nikhil Thorat, Fernanda B. Viégas, Martin Wattenberg, Greg Corrado, Macduff Hughes, and Jeffrey Dean. 2016. Google's multilingual neural machine translation system: Enabling zero-shot translation. *CoRR*, abs/1611.04558.

Minh-Thang Luong, Hieu Pham, and Christopher D. Manning. 2015. Effective approaches to attention-based neural machine translation. *CoRR*, abs/1508.04025.

Rico Sennrich, Barry Haddow, and Alexandra Birch. 2016a. Improving neural machine translation models with monolingual data. In *Proceedings of the 54th Annual Meeting of the Association for Computational Linguistics, ACL 2016, August 7-12, 2016, Berlin, Germany, Volume 1: Long Papers*.

Rico Sennrich, Barry Haddow, and Alexandra Birch. 2016b. Neural machine translation of rare words with subword units. In *Proceedings of the 54th Annual Meeting of the Association for Computational Linguistics (Volume 1: Long Papers)*, pages 1715–1725, Berlin, Germany. Association for Computational Linguistics.

Ashish Vaswani, Noam Shazeer, Niki Parmar, Jakob Uszkoreit, Llion Jones, Aidan N. Gomez, Lukasz Kaiser, and Illia Polosukhin. 2017. Attention is all you need. *CoRR*, abs/1706.03762.

Oriol Vinyals, Ł ukasz Kaiser, Terry Koo, Slav Petrov, Ilya Sutskever, and Geoffrey Hinton. 2015. Grammar as a foreign language. In C. Cortes, N. D. Lawrence, D. D. Lee, M. Sugiyama, and R. Garnett, editors, *Advances in Neural Information Processing Systems 28*, pages 2773–2781. Curran Associates, Inc.

The Ultimate NLP Research Makeup Tutorial: How to Polish your Posters, Slides and Presentations Skills

Gustavo Henrique Paetzold and **Lucia Specia**
Department of Computer Science
University of Sheffield, UK
{g.h.paetzold, l.specia}@sheffield.ac.uk

1 Tutorial Description

There is no question that our research community have, and still has been producing an insurmountable amount of interesting strategies, models and tools to a wide array of problems and challenges in diverse areas of knowledge. But for as long as interesting work has existed, we've been plagued by a great unsolved mystery: how come there is so much interesting work being published in conferences, but not as many interesting and engaging posters and presentations being featured in them? After extensive research and investigation, we think we have finally found cause.

We believe this problem is not being caused directly by our undoubtedly competent researchers themselves, but rather by three organisms which have seemingly infected a great deal of our community:

- **The Style-Eating Bacteria:** Have you ever gotten put off after seeing a large poster made with a basic standard template containing no images, graphs or diagrams illustrating it? It might have been made by a researcher carrying these bacteria.

- **The Character-Replicating Virus:** Every time you've watched an oral presentation featuring slides full of text and formulae which are read in their integrity by the presenter, you met a victim of this virus.

- **The Speech-Jamming Parasite:** The unluckiest among us will have to watch this silent killer ruin our presentations in front of the biggest names in our field. Non-native English speakers and introspective presenters are the most vulnerable targets.

In this tutorial, we present practical and straightforward solutions to researchers who feel like they have been infected by one or more of these ruthless guests. Our tutorial will cover the two main ways through which we present our work to the community: posters and oral presentations.

When it comes to posters, we will introduce various ways through which authors can change the style and content of their posters in order to allow them to draw more attention in those crowded poster sessions. We will use step-by-step examples of poster overhauling to teach attendants how to properly address various issues that are unfortunately commonly found in conference posters in our field, such as bland styling, verbose sections, insufficient illustrating and others.

For oral presentations, we will teach attendants to create slide presentations that not only make it easier to keep the attention of attendants from beginning to end, but also facilitate the life of the presenter in case they do not feel like they have good English proficiency. We will also present some simple techniques that presenters can use to feel more confident during their oral presentations, as well as during the sometimes dreaded "question and answer" session afterwards. A lot of our focus will be turned to non-native English speakers with low speaking proficiency, since we believe those researchers are the ones who have the hardest time during oral presentations.

2 Tutorial Outline

1. **Posters**
   - **Problems:**
     - Unnecessary information
     - Poor section structuring
     - Not enough visuals
     - Too much text
     - Bland styling
   - **Solutions:**

Proceedings of the The 8th International Joint Conference on Natural Language Processing, pages 14–15,
Taipei, Taiwan, November 27 – December 1, 2017. ©2017 AFNLP

- What to remove and what to keep
- Poster sectioning made simple
- How to make things visual:
  * Equations
  * Languages and locations
  * Models and methods
  * Results and findings
  * Other concepts
- Where to find cool poster templates
- Step-by-step poster overhaul

2. **Slide presentations:**
   - **Problems:**
     - Unessential content
     - Verbose sections
     - Poor fluidity
     - Bland styling
   - **Solutions:**
     - What content to exclude
     - Making things more visual
     - Making more dynamic slides
     - Where to find cool slide templates
     - Step-by-step slides overhaul

3. **Oral presentations:**
   - **Problems:**
     - Slide reading
     - Stage fright
     - Lack of confidence
     - Low English proficiency
   - **Solutions:**
     - How to prepare beforehand
     - Summarising your presentation
     - Making and using cue cards
     - Finding a "presentation buddy"

3 Instructors

- **Gustavo Henrique Paetzold:** A Research Associate at the University of Sheffield, UK, who has recently written a Ph.D. thesis on Lexical Simplification for Non-Native English Speakers. His main areas of expertise are Text Simplification and Quality Estimation. Gustavo is currently one of the lead researchers in the SIMPATICO project, which aims to provide novel solutions for Text Simplification, and has received the award for "Best Computer Science Undergraduate Student of 2013" from the State University of Western Paran, as well as the award for "Featured Computer Science Student of 2013" from the Brazilian Society for Computing. Throughout the years of 2013 and 2016, Gustavo has published over 23 papers in conferences and journals, and has already received prizes for some of his presentations.

- **Lucia Specia:** A Professor of Language Engineering and a member of the Natural Language Processing group at the University of Sheffield, UK. Her main areas of research are Machine Translation, Text Adaptation, and Quality Evaluation and Estimation of language output applications. Prof. Specia is the recipient of an ERC Starting Grant on Multimodal Machine Translation (2016-2021) and is currently involved in various other funded research projects, including the European initiatives QT21 (Quality Translation 21), Cracker (Cracking the Language Barrier) and EXPERT (Empirical Methods for Machine Translation). Before joining the University of Sheffield in 2012, she was Senior Lecturer at the University of Wolverhampton, UK (2010- 2011), and research engineer at the Xerox Research Centre, France (2008-2009). She received a PhD in Computer Science from the University of So Paulo, Brazil, in 2008. She has published over 100 research papers in peer-reviewed journals and conference proceedings and organised a number of workshops in the area of Natural Language Processing.

The Challenge of Composition in Distributional and Formal Semantics

Ran Tian
Tohoku University, Japan
tianran@ecei.tohoku.ac.jp

Koji Mineshima
Ochanomizu University, Japan
mineshima.koji@ocha.ac.jp

Pascual Martínez-Goḿez
AIRC, AIST, Japan
pascual.mg@aist.go.jp

1 Tutorial Description

The principle of compositionality states that the meaning of a complete sentence must be explained in terms of the meanings of its subsentential parts; in other words, each syntactic operation should have a corresponding semantic operation. In recent years, it has been increasingly evident that distributional and formal semantics are complementary in addressing composition; while the distributional/vector-based approach can naturally measure semantic similarity (Mitchell and Lapata, 2010), the formal/symbolic approach has a long tradition within logic-based semantic frameworks (Montague, 1974) and can readily be connected to theorem provers or databases to perform complicated tasks. In this tutorial, we will cover recent efforts in extending word vectors to account for composition and reasoning, the various challenging phenomena observed in composition and addressed by formal semantics, and a hybrid approach that combines merits of the two.

For introduction, we briefly review the syntax-semantics interface and word vectors, the two starting points of this tutorial.

Then, we discuss vector-based models for composition, in which word vectors are combined into phrase/sentence vectors according to some syntactic structure (Hashimoto et al., 2014; Pham et al., 2015; Tian et al., 2016). The word vectors and composition operations are jointly learned in an unsupervised manner in these models. We mention but do not focus on approaches disregarding syntax, such as recurrent neural networks.

Next, we move to recent advances in machine learning theory of the most fundamental composition operation, the additive composition (Tian et al., 2017). We explain why additive composition works, how to train additive compositional vectors and how to use them in semantic composition.

As a final part of the vector-based approach, we discuss applications of vector-based composition related to database and reasoning, such as Guu et al. (2015) and Rocktäschel et al. (2015).

We introduce the symbolic approach to composition, also under the principles behind the syntax-semantics interface; its symbolic nature allows the use of theorem provers to perform natural language inferences. As an example, we show how this semantic composition takes place over syntactic derivations in Combinatory Categorial Grammar (CCG) (Steedman, 2000). We also demonstrate how different semantic theories can be implemented over a variety of syntactic grammars (not only CCG) using ccg2lambda (Martínez-Gómez et al., 2016), an open-sourced general framework for compositional semantics.

We then introduce the problem of Recognizing Textual Entailment (RTE) (Dagan et al., 2009), where we test whether a text T entails a hypothesis H. We compare different logic frameworks, including first-order logic, higher-order logic (Mineshima et al., 2015, 2016), and natural logic (Abzianidze, 2015), and discuss semantically challenging constructions such as generalized quantifiers, adjectival modification and intensional operators, drawing on the English dataset FraCaS and the Japanese dataset JSeM for RTE.

The solution to many RTE problems requires the use of external linguistic knowledge such as synonyms, antonyms, and paraphrases. Since vector representations naturally encode semantic similarities between words and phrases, here we expect a great synergy between the formal and distributional approaches. In the closing section of this tutorial, we introduce a widely adopted hybrid approach toward RTE, in which semantic similarities between words and phrases are explicitly converted to logic rules as linguistic knowledge used in inference (Tian et al., 2014; Beltagy et al., 2016;

Proceedings of the The 8th International Joint Conference on Natural Language Processing, pages 16–17,
Taipei, Taiwan, November 27 – December 1, 2017. ©2017 AFNLP

Martínez-Gómez et al., 2017). This approach has the merit that all knowledge is explicit, and it can easily integrate existing linguistic ontologies such as WordNet. We demonstrate how the distributional approach can overcome the low coverage of linguistic resources by composing phrase vectors faithful to meaning and compatible with logic, and how the formal approach can reduce computational complexity in logical inference by identifying the need of linguistic knowledge between specific concepts and constructing axioms on-demand.

2 Tutorial Outline

- Introduction
  - The syntax-semantics interface
  - Word vectors
- Vector-based approach
  - Vector-based composition models
  - Theory of additive composition
  - Vector-based reasoning
- Symbolic approach
  - ccg2lambda: compositionality for your favorite semantic theory
  - Logic systems for RTE
  - RTE datasets for formal semantics: FraCaS and JSeM
- A hybrid approach toward RTE

Ran Tian is a Project Assistant Professor at Tohoku University. He works on theory of vector-based composition, and integration of distributional semantics into logical inference.

Koji Mineshima is a Project Associate Professor at Ochanomizu University. He is working on Formal Semantics, Logic and Computational Linguistics. His recent work has focused on CCG semantic parsing, anaphora resolution and recognizing textual entailment.

Pascual Martínez-Gómez is a Research Scientist at the Artificial Intelligence Research Center, AIRC-AIST. He investigates extensions of tree transducers and their applications to recognizing textual entailment, fact validation and question-answering over large knowledge bases.

References

L. Abzianidze. 2015. A tableau prover for natural logic and language. In *EMNLP*.

I. Beltagy, S. Roller, P. Cheng, K. Erk, and R. J. Mooney. 2016. Representing meaning with a combination of logical and distributional models. *Computational Linguistics*, 42(4).

I. Dagan, B. Dolan, B. Magnini, and D. Roth. 2009. Recognizing textual entailment: Rational, evaluation and approaches. *Natural Language Engineering*, 15.

K. Guu, J. Miller, and P. Liang. 2015. Traversing knowledge graphs in vector space. In *EMNLP*.

K. Hashimoto, P. Stenetorp, M. Miwa, and Y. Tsuruoka. 2014. Jointly learning word representations and composition functions using predicate-argument structures. In *EMNLP*.

P. Martínez-Gómez, K. Mineshima, Y. Miyao, and D. Bekki. 2016. ccg2lambda: A compositional semantics system. In *ACL*.

P. Martínez-Gómez, K. Mineshima, Y. Miyao, and D. Bekki. 2017. On-demand injection of lexical knowledge for recognising textual entailment. In *EACL*.

K. Mineshima, P. Martínez-Gómez, Y. Miyao, and D. Bekki. 2015. Higher-order logical inference with compositional semantics. In *EMNLP*.

K. Mineshima, R. Tanaka, P. Martínez-Gómez, Y. Miyao, and D. Bekki. 2016. Building compositional semantics and higher-order inference system for a wide-coverage Japanese CCG parser. In *EMNLP*.

J. Mitchell and M. Lapata. 2010. Composition in distributional models of semantics. *Cognitive Science*, 34(8).

R. Montague. 1974. English as a formal language. In R. Montague, editor, *Formal philosophy*. Yale University Press.

N. T. Pham, G. Kruszewski, A. Lazaridou, and M. Baroni. 2015. Jointly optimizing word representations for lexical and sentential tasks with the c-phrase model. In *ACL*.

T. Rocktäschel, S. Singh, and S. Riedel. 2015. Injecting logical background knowledge into embeddings for relation extraction. In *NAACL*.

M. Steedman. 2000. *The Syntactic Process*. MIT Press.

R. Tian, Y. Miyao, and T. Matsuzaki. 2014. Logical inference on dependency-based compositional semantics. In *ACL*.

R. Tian, N. Okazaki, and K. Inui. 2016. Learning semantically and additively compositional distributional representations. In *ACL*.

R. Tian, N. Okazaki, and K. Inui. 2017. The mechanism of additive composition. *Machine Learning*.

Author Index

Association for Computational Linguistics
209 N. Eighth Street
Stroudsburg, Pennsylvania 18360

ISBN 978-1-5108-5296-9

CURRAN ASSOCIATES INC.
proceedings.com